About the

Changing Our World Series

In every generation, there are people who change our world with important contributions in fields such as science, politics, and the arts. These women and men often challenge others' ideas and have the courage to fight for their own beliefs. Sometimes this fight can mean great personal suffering, or even the loss of their own lives.

Changing Our World books are about some of the people from the twentieth century who have changed the world. Although they are very different from one another, they share one important trait: the determination to succeed. Their accomplishments will last for many generations to come.

Be sure to read all the books in the Changing Our World series:

Alvin Ailey, Jr.

Benazir Bhutto

Stephen Biko

Barbara Bush

Dian Fossey

Mikhail Gorbachev

Colin Powell

H. Norman Schwarzkopf

CHANGING OUR WORLD

COLIN POWELL

Jonathan Everston

with

Andrea Raab

A BANTAM SKYLARK BOOK®
NEW YORK • TORONTO • LONDON • SYDNEY • AUCKLAND

This book is dedicated to Dr. Thomas Bulger, my literary mentor, and Winifred Foy, a lifelong source of inspiration—J.E.

RL 3, 007-011

COLIN POWELL

A Bantam Skylark Book/September 1991

Skylark Books is a registered trademark of Bantam Books, a division of Bantam Doubleday Dell Publishing Group, Inc.
Registered in U.S. Patent and Trademark Office and elsewhere.

Produced by Angel Entertainment, Inc.
Cover design by Joseph DePinho

ISBN 0-553-15966-6

Published simultaneously in the United States and Canada

Bantam Books are published by Bantam Books, a division of Bantam Doubleday Dell Publishing Group, Inc. Its trademark, consisting of the words "Bantam Books" and the portrayal of a rooster, is Registered in U.S. Patent and Trademark Office and in other countries. Marca Registrada. Bantam Books, 666 Fifth Avenue, New York, New York 10103.

PRINTED IN THE UNITED STATES OF AMERICA
OPM 0 9 8 7 6 5 4 3 2 1

Contents

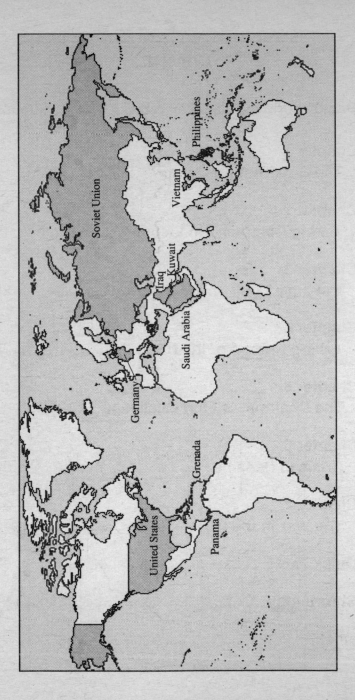

United States of America

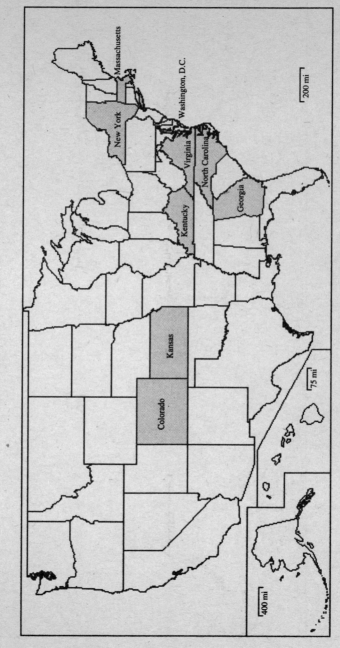

Background

During World War II, United States President Franklin D. Roosevelt and Prime Minister Winston Churchill of England met to discuss how to plan their allied invasion against Germany, Japan, and Italy (known as the Axis). They decided to create a commanding group, called the combined chiefs of staff. The chiefs of staff would be made up of the leaders of both English and American armed services. These chiefs would plan the battle strategies for the U.S. and British troops. President Roosevelt then named the U.S. service chiefs—the Army chief of staff, the commanding general of the U.S. Fleet, and the chief of Naval Operations—to the combined chiefs of staff.

The combined chiefs of staff immediately took over the planning of the war strategy, including all operations for the Army and Navy. President Roosevelt soon added a chairman to the American staff. The president wanted one person to keep him informed of developments in the battlefield.

When the Allies successfully beat the Axis, and the U.S. won an impressive victory at the end of World War II, the combined chiefs of staff were praised highly for their role in the victory. They had provided detailed military direction for both American and English troops. They had also kept the president and the prime minister fully informed on military operations. President Harry Truman told the chiefs of staff chairman at that time that the South could have won the American Civil War if they had had a military organization like the American representatives on the combined chiefs of staff.

In 1947, with President Truman's support, Congress passed the National Security Act. The act established the American chiefs of staff as a permanent organization within the national defense system. The staff was called the Joint Chiefs of Staff (JCS). The new organization was given a staff of one hundred officers. Their responsibilities included preparing strategies and providing training and education for all of the armed services.

In 1949 a military chairman position was set up to run the JCS permanently during times of peace as well as during wartime. The chairman would be an officer who had over thirty years experience. He would be appointed by the president, with the consent of the Senate, to serve a two-year term. He could be reappointed once. His immediate boss would be the secretary of defense.

In 1986 the Goldwater-Nichols Reorganization Act placed the Joint Chiefs of Staff chairman on a higher level than the other service chiefs. He was also given his own staff of 1,600 people, as well as authority over the other joint chiefs. He became the most powerful military officer in the United States.

Today the Joint Chiefs of Staff consists of the heads of the Army, Navy, Air Force, and Marines, the chairman, and vice chairman. They meet three times a week at the Pentagon in Washington, D.C., in a specially designed, windowless room called "The Tank." Their meetings are closed to the public and conducted in the utmost secrecy. The JCS has many responsibilities. In addition to being the military advisers to the secretary of defense, the National Security Council, Congress, and the president, they also plan the defense budget (the amount of money that can be spent on military protection, aid, and research programs) and combat command plans.

The JCS works closely with the president, the secretary of defense, and the field commander to plan and execute all military operations during wartime. No military move takes place without many long hours of intense discussion and planning, with the chairman heading all meetings.

General Colin L. Powell was appointed JCS chairman in 1989. At fifty-three, he became the youngest chairman ever. He was also the first black chairman and the only one to rise to the nation's highest military office without graduating from a military academy.

In 1990 the Persian Gulf crisis brought Chairman Powell into the public eye. Never before had a Joint Chiefs of Staff chairman played such a dominant role during wartime. With quiet authority, Colin led the allies to a decisive victory in the gulf. And back home in America the boy from the Bronx, who had not been sure what career to choose, became a hero to millions of Americans. This is the story of his life.

1

The Boy from the Bronx

Hundreds of soldiers cheered as the sleek military plane landed at the Saudi Arabian air base. It was just before Christmas, 1990, but the temperature in the desert had soared into the nineties. The soldiers were men and women of the United States Air Force who were training for a possible air assault against the country of Iraq. The plane in front of them carried a man whose decisions might soon change their lives and affect the whole world. That man was four-star general Colin L. Powell, chairman of the United States' Joint Chiefs of Staff.

The soldiers saluted Colin as he stepped out of the plane. For many of them, his visit brought much needed motivation. The soldiers had been practicing their mission since arriving in Saudi Arabia on August 8. That was only six days after Iraqi President Saddam Hussein had ordered three divisions of his massive army to invade the tiny, oil-rich country of Kuwait.

American forces had come to Saudi Arabia, along with troops from many other nations, to force Iraq's dictator to withdraw from Kuwait. They had been rehearsing in the intense heat of the desert for a war that many people hoped would never take place. The soldiers had worked long and hard during their four-and-a-half months of training.

Out of respect for the religious customs of their host country, they had not been permitted to do things that American soldiers often relied upon to help them through their homesickness and stress. The soldiers were not allowed to drink beer and male soldiers could not pin up posters of pretty girls around the barracks. Christian and Jewish religious services had to be conducted practically in secret. This was because Saudi Arabia is a strict Muslim country and its leaders did not want the soldiers to practice their non-Muslim faiths publicly.

Women soldiers stationed in Saudi Arabia were having an especially hard time with the restrictions.

They could not appear in public wearing their short-sleeved uniforms, since by Muslim standards this was not considered modest behavior for women. If an American female soldier wanted to travel anywhere in the country, she had to cover herself with the long, flowing veils worn by Arab women. She also had to have a male soldier escort her.

On top of these difficulties, the soldiers awaiting General Powell knew that Christmas and the holidays were coming soon. None of them wanted to spend it sitting in a military mess tent, brushing sand off of their Christmas turkey!

As Colin Powell stood before the soldiers, he was aware that he was overseeing an operation that might cost thousands of human lives. He had always been able to inspire military people of all ranks to place their trust in him, and that was what he hoped for now.

Although no formal declaration of war had been made, and many people were still hoping for a peaceful solution to the conflict in the Middle East, Colin wanted his troops to know that if war did come, the United States would fight for victory.

He began speaking, and his voice boomed through the still desert air. "When we launch this attack, we will launch it violently, we will launch it massively, so there will be no doubt when it's over who won."

The soldiers' cheers were loud enough to drown out the roar of the engine of an F-15 jet fighter.

Colin Luther Powell was born on April 5, 1937, in Harlem, which is a part of New York City. When Colin was three, and his older sister, Marilyn, was eight-and-a-half, his family moved to the South Bronx. They lived in an apartment house at 952 Kelly Street. Colin's father earned his living as a garment factory shipping foreman, and his mother also worked in the garment business as a seamstress.

Colin grew up playing stickball and "soldier" with his friends on Kelly Street. He had a part-time job fixing baby carriages and cribs for a furniture store on Westchester Avenue to earn money after school. The furniture store was owned by Jewish people, and while he worked there Colin learned to speak a little bit of Yiddish. Years later when Colin was a Pentagon aide, he often liked to use Yiddish expressions when speaking with colleagues.

Colin says that his first heroes were his parents—Luther Theophilus Powell and Maud Ariel Powell. They had come to New York from Jamaica in the

1920s, and moved in with relatives or close friends whom they called "aunts" or "cousins." Luther and Maud Powell spoke English with a lilting West Indies accent, and proudly considered themselves British subjects before they became Americans. While Luther Powell was self-educated, Maud Powell had graduated from high school. Colin says that sometimes when his mother became annoyed with his father, she would remind him of this fact.

Church played an important role in the family's life. The Powells first belonged to the Anglican church of the West Indies, which strongly emphasized formal ritual and prayer. Later they became members of the Episcopal church. For a while, Colin was an altar boy at St. Margaret's Episcopal Church on 151st Street in the Bronx.

Education was also very important to the Powells. Colin's cousin, Grace Watson, recalls, "We came from families who dreamed for you, who demanded achievement, and who believed you must not waste yourself." Colin himself explains, "It was unthinkable in the family not to do something. Doing it didn't mean becoming a brain surgeon. It just meant getting educated, getting a job, and going as far as you could with that job."

For Colin, however, it would take some time before his life's goals would become clear to him. Despite his parents' insistence that Colin study hard, he did not do all that well in school. In high school he spent much of his time with his friends—playing stickball, racing bicycles down Kelly Street, and eating hamburgers at the local White Castle. Colin also joined the Morris High School track team, and often practiced running in nearby Van Cortland Park.

Colin just did not like to work hard at certain things when he was growing up. He remembers sleeping late one morning while everyone else in his house was doing chores. His mother became so annoyed that she made Colin's four-year-old cousin pour a glass of cold water on his head in order to wake him up.

After Colin's graduation from high school in 1954, Colin was not sure what he wanted to do with his life. He knew, however, that his parents expected him to go to college. He was accepted to both New York University and the City College of New York, but NYU was too expensive. At City College Colin started out thinking he would be an engineering major. But one day when the professor posed a mathematical problem that was too complicated for him to figure out,

Colin decided he'd be better off trying to tackle something more solid. He chose geology—the study of the earth.

In America during the 1950s, when Colin was in college, prejudice against black people limited many of the education and job opportunities available to them. Few black people were able to attend college, and many companies did not hire blacks for high-paying jobs. Some companies did not hire blacks at all.

The Army's ROTC (Reserve Officers Training Corps) program on college campuses did not discriminate on the basis of race. They accepted all students who were interested in serving in the armed forces. To Colin this seemed like a good opportunity and he joined ROTC. The Army promised advanced training, and a secure and steady job after graduation. But this is not the only thing that attracted Colin. He liked the black uniforms with the brass buttons that the ROTC students wore and was impressed by the smartly dressed young men marching through the campus. He also noticed that many of the pretty girls on campus were impressed, too.

Once he was a member of ROTC, Colin joined the Pershing Rifles, a rifle drill team named after the famous World War I general, Jack Pershing. He was soon appointed commander of the Pershing Rifles. As commander he recruited new members and encouraged the group to work hard. Under Colin's eyes, the Pershing Rifle Drill Squad drilled relentlessly on the school grounds. He worked them hard to get them into shape for the big annual drill meet that coming spring. There they would test their skills against those of twenty other schools.

That year the Pershing Rifles went into the meet raring to go. When it was over, the squad was awarded the highest scores ever recorded. It was Colin Powell's first public display of his ability to command troops.

At the end of his fourth year Colin became an ROTC cadet colonel, the highest rank, and was named a "distinguished military graduate." It took Colin another half year to finish college, including one summer session. But he did graduate—with a straight C average. He admits that he was able to graduate mainly because he got all A's in his military courses. Colin now says he doesn't know if he would have finished college at all had it not been for his involvement in ROTC.

Colin's parents did not object to his joining the military in college. They figured that he would proba-

---

Reserve Officers Training Corps

The ROTC program was established by the National Defense Act of 1916 to prepare young men for the possibility of war. This act also created the Officers Reserve Corp (ORC) to which ROTC graduates were assigned on graduation. The ROTC consists of a senior division and a junior division. The senior division is organized at universities and colleges requiring four years of study for a degree and the junior division consists of public or private military schools. ROTC students, as they are called, take military courses, such as military science, military tactics, and leadership classes. Besides classwork, ROTC students participate in many training programs, daily workouts and maneuvers, and field training exercises. ROTC classes go on field trips, where they learn to use weapons, march in the woods, and learn navigation. These field trips are based on the programs being followed by active Army units. Educational opportunities exist for ROTC students after graduation, ranging from officer candidates school through the Army War College. ROTC students can also get good jobs in the service after graduation. Today ROTC programs give students a free education in exchange for four years of military service to their country.

---

bly get drafted anyway, since young American men were still being drafted into military service in the 1950s. But they certainly did not think that he would

Colin's college graduation photograph in 1958. (Courtesy of City College)

spend his life in the Army. They expected Colin to become an officer, serve for a three-year "tour," or military job assignment, then get out of the Army, and find a good civilian job. They did not anticipate that Colin would never want to get out—at least, not before he reached the very top.

2

Taking Command in Vietnam

On June 9, 1958, shortly after his graduation from City College, Colin proudly received his golden "butter bars," the brass insignia of rank worn by all Army second lieutenants. He also began earning a salary of sixty dollars a week as an infantry officer. He left New York for summer training at the Infantry Officer Basic Course, given at Fort Bragg, North Carolina.

Infantry training at Fort Bragg was very difficult. Infantry is the branch of the army that specializes in ground combat. The training days began at "O-dark-thirty," which means long before the sun comes up, and ended after midnight. Colin received basic instruction in military discipline, the use of weapons,

How the U.S. Army Is Organized

Squad—a unit of six to twelve soldiers, usually commanded by a sergeant.

Section—contains fifteen to thirty soldiers and is led by a sergeant.

Platoon—consists of three to four squads and is usually led by a lieutenant and a sergeant.

Company—consists of three to six platoons and is usually led by a captain.

Troop—a company-sized unit of cavalry.

Battery—a company-sized group of artillery pieces.

Battalion—consists of three to six companies, usually commanded by a lieutenant colonel.

Squadron—a battalion-sized unit of armored cavalry.

Regiment—consists of three to six battalions usually commanded by a colonel.

Brigade—consists of three to six battalions and is commanded either by a colonel or a brigadier general.

Division—consists of three brigades or regiments, plus some companies or battalions as supporting units, and is usually commanded by a major general.

Corps—contains several divisions, plus smaller supporting units, and is usually commanded by a lieutenant general.

Army—consists of several corps, plus smaller supporting units, and is usually commanded by a four-star general.

troop management, first aid, and riot control. Following his graduation from the Officer Basic Course, Colin then traveled to Fort Benning, Georgia. There he attended Airborne school and learned how to parachute out of airplanes. He also went to Ranger school, where he underwent an intensive combat survival course. Long, fast runs, hand-to-hand combat in sawdust pits, lessons in tracking enemies, and setting ambushes in the woods were all part of the challenging Ranger course. As Colin remembered from ROTC, being in the Army involved a lot more than just wearing fancy uniforms and marching in parades—it was very hard work! But by the time he had completed his courses, he felt like a genuine infantry officer.

Colin's next stop was an American Army base in West Germany. He was now ready to take on his first real duty assignment—as a platoon leader in Company B, Second Armored Rifle Battalion, Forty-eighth Infantry, United States Army, Europe. He served there for two years, and was then transferred to Fort Devens, Massachusetts, where he was second-in-command of Company A, First Battle Group, Fourth Infantry.

While Colin was at Fort Devens, he met a young

woman named Alma Vivian Johnson on a blind date. She was from Birmingham, Alabama. Before long the two fell deeply in love. On August 25, 1962 Colin and Alma were married. Only a few short months later, Colin was shipped out to a country halfway across the world—Vietnam.

Since the late 1950s, the Communist country of North Vietnam had been attempting to take over its neighbor, South Vietnam. The United States did not want the communists to gain power in South Vietnam, so the American government sent in a group of military advisers to help the South Vietnamese try to stop them. By mid-1962 the number of American advisers in South Vietnam had increased from 700 to 12,000. By the end of 1963 the number totaled 15,000. And Colin Powell—who by that time had been promoted to the rank of captain—was one of those advisers.

When Colin left for Vietnam, he was still a very young man. He was also a married man who would shortly become a father. But as sorry as he was to leave his family, Colin felt excited about finally getting to see some real "action." He later explained: "It was what infantry officers should want, so I was looking forward to it. I was twenty-four years old then, and this was hot stuff."

Vietnam

Vietnam is a country in Southeast Asia. The country is split into two states: the Republic of Vietnam (called South Vietnam) and the Democratic Republic of Vietnam (called North Vietnam). The capital of South Vietnam is Saigon; the capital of North Vietnam is Hanoi.

China ruled Vietnam for over a thousand years until the French took control in 1883. During World War II Japan defeated the French government in Vietnam and allowed the Vietnamese to proclaim their independence. The Vietnamese communists set up their government in North Vietnam. After Japan was defeated in World War II, the French moved back into South Vietnam. In 1946 North Vietnam attacked South Vietnam so that they could make the whole country Communist. The U.S. sent military advisers to South Vietnam in the 1950s to help them defend against the North Vietnamese. In 1954 the war ended when neither side was able to win. But the fighting started up again in the 1960s and America again sent advisers and later troops. By 1973 it was clear that the U.S. could not help the South Vietnamese defeat the North Vietnamese. U.S. troops left the country and South Vietnam was defeated in 1975.

After Colin left, Alma moved back home to Birmingham to stay with her family during her pregnancy. When the Powells' first child—a son named

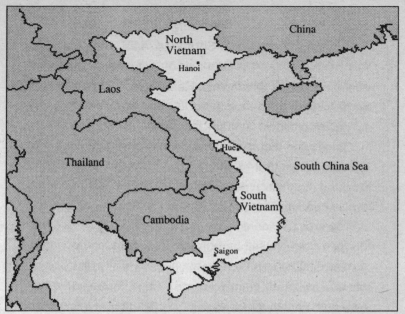

Vietnam and Southeast Asia

Michael—was born, Colin was leading a combat unit near the North Vietnamese border. The news that his wife had given birth did not reach him for three weeks.

A few months later, while leading his unit through a rice paddy, Colin stepped on a punji-stick trap that was hidden just beneath the surface of the flooded paddy. The razor-sharp bamboo stick entered his left sole with such force that it came out the top of his foot. Colin immediately was sent for treatment to a hospital in the South Vietnamese city of Hue. He recovered in a few weeks, and went right back on patrol.

The Purple Heart and Bronze Star for Valor

The Purple Heart and the Bronze Star for Valor are two awards given to soldiers who distinguish themselves during wartime. The Purple Heart is the most highly respected decoration of the U.S. Armed Forces. It is earned by any soldier wounded in combat. The oldest military decoration, it was descended from George Washington's Badge of Merit, which was awarded for gallantry and service. The award is a purple heart within a bronze border bearing a profile head of George Washington in military uniform.

The Bronze Star for Valor is awarded to any soldier who distinguishes himself by heroism in surface combat or by outstanding achievement in connection with military operations against an enemy. The award is a one-and-a-half inch bronze star with a smaller bronze star in the center. The award is hung with a red, white, and blue ribbon.

Colin received two medals during this tour of duty—a Bronze Star for Valor and a Purple Heart. They would be the first of many awarded to him throughout his career.

After a year in Vietnam, Colin was sent back to the United States to become a test officer for the U.S. Army Infantry Board at Fort Benning, Georgia. Before taking his new position, however, he traveled to Alabama to see Alma, and to meet his baby son. It was a very emotional reunion, especially since Colin would soon have to leave again.

Colin's homecoming was emotional for another reason. By the early 1960s the nation was caught up in the Civil Rights Movement. In some parts of the country, especially in the South, it was as if two separate societies existed—one for black people and one for white people. Blacks were forbidden to attend white schools or churches, to eat in the same restaurants as whites, to sit beside whites on trains and buses, to drink from the same water fountains, and to use the same public restrooms. Black people wanted one society—one in which people of all races were treated equally under the law. But many white people did not want to give up any of their rights or privileges. As a result, violent fights broke out between black people and white people. This violence occurred in many towns throughout the South.

Colin was shocked and horrified by the race riots taking place in Birmingham. "Police dogs, bombs, water cannons, mobs, and cattle prods were being used to suppress blacks who were determined to exercise their fundamental rights . . ." he later wrote.

In the military, black and white soldiers were usually treated more equally. Colin was not used to such blatant racism. One day when he stopped at a hamburger shop to get some lunch, the waitress refused to serve him because he was black. He was also stopped on an Alabama highway by a police patrol. The officer was giving out bumper stickers that urged people to vote for Barry Goldwater for president. Colin's car had New York license plates and a bumper sticker that supported President Johnson. The officer looked over Colin and his car and said, "Boy, get out of here. You are not smart enough to hang around." Colin still looks back on these incidents with pain and anger.

During the four years that Colin spent at Fort Benning, the situation in Vietnam got worse. By the end of 1968, 550,000 American troops had been sent to South Vietnam. American soldiers were being killed in battle every day, and many people in the United States were losing confidence in the president's reasons for keeping the conflict going. Some began to protest openly against the war. Young people were especially loud in their protests. Students marched with signs on college campuses throughout the country. As the American casualties increased, the U.S. became more convinced that the war could not be won.

Helicopters were used extensively by the United States in the Vietnam War. They allowed soldiers to hover in the air while attacking enemy ground troops with gunfire. (AP/Wide World, 1989)

In 1967 Colin went to the United States Army Command and General Staff College at Fort Leavenworth, Kansas, where he learned the art of command and decision-making. During this time, he decided that he wanted to go to graduate school. But his commanding officer told him that his college record was not good enough. Angered by this comment, Colin buckled down and graduated second in his class of 1,244.

Graduate school would have to wait, though. Colin returned to Vietnam in June 1968. He had recently been promoted to major, and his wife had given birth to their second child, a girl named Linda. Now he found himself again fighting in the hot, steamy jungles of Vietnam.

Sometimes Colin's tour of duty in Vietnam was dangerous. One day when he was out on a helicopter mission, the pilot tried to land in a small jungle clearing. As the pilot started down, Colin knew that they were in trouble. The pilot lost control and the helicopter suddenly shifted to the left. Colin watched as the rotor blade struck a tree and stopped. He bent over and put his hands under his knees and prepared for the crash.

"When we crashed, I didn't think about anything else but leaving," Colin recalls. "I hit the [seatbelt], jumped out, and ran a few feet. Then I turned around and realized the helicopter was starting to smoke while the men were still in there. I ran back and got the division commander out. He was barely conscious. He had a fractured shoulder. I pulled him out and others carried him away. I went back in and got the chief of staff out. He had a concussion. Then I went back to get an aide, who we thought was dead . . . We got him out and pulled off his helmet. It was all bent out of shape, but it had saved his life . . . The pilot we also got out; his back was fractured."

Members of the First Air Cavalry Division fire at enemy positions near Saigon during the Vietnam War. (AP/Wide World, 1969)

For this act of bravery, Colin received the Soldier's Medal, awarded to soldiers whose heroism does not involve actual combat with an enemy. Colin, however, did not look upon his actions as especially heroic. He felt he was merely doing his duty. But years later others would remember him for his quick thinking, excellent command, and brave actions in Vietnam.

3

Making a Mark on Washington

Colin returned to the United States in July 1969. He finally got his wish to go to graduate school that fall, on a full Army scholarship. He went to business school at George Washington University, in Washington, D.C. He received an A in every course, except for one B. Colin believed that the lessons he learned in business school about how to run an organization well would be helpful to him in his Army career. "Commanding a unit also means managing it efficiently," he once explained.

During this period, Colin was promoted to lieutenant colonel. His wife Alma also gave birth to their third child, a daughter they named Annemarie.

In 1972 Colin was one of seventeen people

chosen from among 1,500 military and civilian appli-
cants for the prestigious White House Fellows program. This program is designed to introduce talented
young professionals to the inner workings of government.

"The unusual part of my career really started as
a White House fellow," Colin said later. He suddenly
went from being an unknown lieutenant colonel to
receiving lessons on how decisions were made at the
White House. Possibly because of his business
school background, Colin was assigned to the White
House Office of Management and Budget. At that
time it was run by a man named Caspar Weinberger,
and his deputy, Frank C. Carlucci. These two men
would remain very important friends to Colin throughout his career.

The fellowship program lasted for one year. Then
Colin went off to Korea to serve as a battalion commander. A year later he returned to Washington,
where he spent the next seven years serving as a
military aide in the Defense Department.

In 1981 Ronald Reagan became president of the
United States and another opportunity was presented
to Colin. Caspar Weinberger had been appointed
President Reagan's secretary of defense, and Frank

Carlucci was once again Weinberger's deputy. Colin, who had been promoted to brigadier general in 1979, had stayed in touch with both men over the years. Now he was invited to become military assistant to the secretary of defense.

As military assistant, Colin's job was to deal with any international problems that developed. But while he was keeping busy with international affairs, a problem was brewing at home. This problem would come to be known as the Iran-contra scandal.

In the summer of 1985 Congress found out that the president's national security adviser, a Navy admiral named John Poindexter, had asked Colin for information about an antitank missile called the TOW. Admiral Poindexter wanted to know how much TOW missiles cost, and how many of them were available. He told Colin that he wanted to send the weapons to Iran, to help that country fight a war against Iraq. Neither Colin nor Secretary of Defense Weinberger agreed with Admiral Poindexter's plan. Iran was a country known to practice terrorism, and Congress had made it illegal to sell weapons to the Iranians in 1979.

But Admiral Poindexter had very complicated reasons for wanting to sell the missiles to Iran. Islamic

The Iran–Iraq War (1980 – 1988)

In 1979 the Shah of Iran was driven out of his country by a revolution. This ended twenty-five centuries of rule by Persian kings. The new government was controlled by leaders of the Islamic faith who made harsh rules for Iranians to live by, and said that other Arab countries should do the same. This threatened Iraq in particular because its leader, Saddam Hussein, had no intention of sharing power with religious leaders of his country. Although Iran's population was three times larger than Iraq's, Saddam knew that Iran was weakened by its recent revolution. On September 17, 1980 he started a war that would eventually kill over a million people. But Iran fought back with unexpected strength and managed to capture large portions of Iraq. After nearly winning the war, Iran started to run out of men and weapons. Finally, in 1988, the two exhausted countries agreed to a United Nations demand to stop fighting. Iran and Iraq are still bitter enemies.

terrorists had taken a group of Americans hostage, and were still holding them captive in Lebanon. Members of President Reagan's administration believed that if the United States secretly sold Iran the weapons they wanted, the terrorists might let the hostages go free.

The Iranians were also willing to pay a lot of money for the TOW missiles, and the Reagan administration needed that money for a specific reason. They intended to pay for the military operations of a group of rebels who opposed the Communist leaders of Nicaragua, a country in Central America. These rebels were called *contras*. The problem was that Congress had not approved sending money to the contras.

Many people were outraged at the Iran-contra situation because it seemed as if the president and members of his administration were trying to run their own government, without the involvement of Congress. This went completely against America's democratic system, which is based on the belief that citizens have the right to determine the actions of their government.

Although Colin was personally against selling weapons to Iran, he felt he had to obey the orders of his superiors. So he did. Still, Colin made sure to write a memo to Admiral Poindexter. He reminded him that he really was supposed to tell Congress about his plans before carrying them out. Later, when the members of Congress finally learned about Colin's warning to the admiral about the weapons deal, they praised him as an honorable man.

In June 1986 Colin left Washington, D.C., to

return to his first love—commanding troops. The Army sent him back to West Germany to command the V Corps, an important unit of 75,000 soldiers stationed near the city of Frankfurt. Colin said his new job made him "probably the happiest general in the world."

But six months later Colin received a long-distance telephone call from his old friend, Frank Carlucci. The Iran-contra scandal had forced Admiral Poindexter to resign from his position, and President Reagan had chosen Carlucci as his new national security adviser. Frank wanted Colin to come back to Washington and become his deputy national security adviser. Colin's answer was simple. He said, "No way."

When Frank Carlucci called to ask Colin again, his answer was still no. After Carlucci called a third time, he realized it was going to take something very special to convince Colin to take the job.

The following night Colin's phone rang. On the other end of the line was President Reagan. "I know you've been looking forward to this command," said the president. "But we need you here."

Frank Carlucci had known that Colin would never refuse a personal request from his commander in chief. "Mr. President," Colin responded, "I'm a soldier, and if I can help, I'll come." With that, Colin packed his bags and returned to Washington.

4

Taking Charge of the NSC

Soon after Colin returned to Washington, he and Alma received the most painful news of their lives. They learned that their son, Michael, a twenty-four-year-old Army first lieutenant stationed in Germany, had been riding in a jeep when the driver lost control. The jeep had turned over, Michael had lost twenty-two pints of blood, and his pelvis had been broken in six places. Doctors told the Powells they didn't know if Michael would live, but if he did, he would probably be confined to a wheelchair for the rest of his life.

Four days later Michael was flown to Walter Reed Army Medical Center in Washington for a series of intensive operations. Colin stayed at his son's bedside the entire time. "You'll make it," he promised

Michael. "You want to make it, so you will make it!"

As Colin had predicted, Michael survived the operations, and temporarily moved back home with his parents. Physical therapists worked with him for weeks at the Powells' home in Fort Meyer, Virginia. But the best medicine for Michael seemed to have been his father simply telling him over and over, "You'll make it."

Sixteen months after the accident, Michael was able to walk with a cane. He married his college sweetheart, was released from his Army duties, and took a job as a civilian employee in the office of the secretary of defense.

Some months before, in December 1987, Caspar Weinberger had decided to resign his position as secretary of defense. His wife had become very ill, and needed him to help take care of her. After Weinberger left, Frank Carlucci was appointed President Reagan's new secretary of defense, and Colin was asked to take Carlucci's place as the president's

---

Colin's Children

Michael, 28, an employee in the Defense Department, is married with a two-year-old son; Linda, 25, is an actress living in New York; Annemarie, 20, is a student at William and Mary College in Virginia.

Colin being named national security adviser on November 5, 1987. Behind Colin from left: Defense Secretary Caspar Weinberger, President Reagan and former National Security Adviser Frank Carlucci. (UPI/Bettman)

new national security adviser. It was the first time in the history of the United States that a black person had been given this senior White House position.

Some people felt it was significant that a black person had been chosen for such a high position in Washington's bureaucracy. But Colin did not want the fact that he was black to be given so much attention. He wanted his achievements to be recognized instead. At the same time Colin was quick to praise the black soldiers who had paved the way for his advancement. Colin told members of the women's auxiliary of the James Reese Europe American Legion—Washington's oldest black patriotic group—that they should all be grateful to the segregated units that had come before him. The soldiers had not had the same opportunities to advance, but they had worked just as hard as he had. Colin reminded the group that day, and continues to remind others, to "not let the torch drop." Even though he had risen to high positions in the military and the government, Colin still wanted to increase opportunities for the advancement of other black soldiers.

In his new job as head of the National Security Council (NSC), Colin began work each day at 7:00 in the morning, and did not leave his office until 7:00 o'clock at night. He would start the day by meeting with the secretary of state and the secretary of defense.

The secretary of state is the person in American government responsible for handling America's relationships with foreign countries. The secretary of defense is in charge of making sure that America's military forces are qualified and ready to defend the

Black People in the Military

Black people have always served in the American military, but they have not always been treated equally. Since the arrival of the first black people in America as slaves in 1619, they have been called upon to defend the nation. In 1639 white leaders began to fear that slaves carrying arms would revolt so blacks were excluded from military service.

By the middle of 1862, during the Civil War, black regiments were formed because white volunteers were scarce. The Emancipation Proclamation, which officially freed the slaves in 1863, contained a provision for the enlistment of blacks. After the war President Lincoln said that the North might not have won without the help of the 390,000 black soldiers who had fought.

Over 200,000 black soldiers served during World War I, but they were still kept separate from the white troops. Most of the black soldiers did not see any combat duty. Instead they did manual labor. At the beginning of World War II, about seventy-eight percent of the 700,000 black soldiers were still segregated and used for manual labor. Again, the shortages of white troops forced the use of more blacks on the front lines.

President Truman signed an order in 1948, ending the separation of whites and blacks in the military. By the end of the Korean War over ninety percent of all black soldiers were placed in integrated units.

Today more blacks hold management positions in the military than they do in civilian corporations.

country. Colin and the secretaries would discuss foreign policy plans concerning what was happening in different parts of the world, such as Central America, the Far East, the Persian Gulf, or the Soviet Union.

Afterwards Colin would meet with President Reagan to brief, or inform, him of what he and the secretaries had talked about, and to offer the NSC's recommendations on what decisions the president ought to make. Colin would usually spend about three hours a day speaking with President Reagan. When Colin and the president were not speaking directly to each other, they were always linked by twenty-four-hour-a-day telephone access. Colin's responsibilities as national security adviser also included consulting with members of Congress on Capitol Hill, giving briefings on the National Security Council's activities to the press, and working with the NSC's staff.

Colin liked his new job, although he often felt pressured by the long hours and constant responsibilities. Since an international crisis could occur at any time of the day or night, Colin always had to be prepared. He often took work home with him at night and on weekends. But he still tried to keep his home life and professional life separate by not dis-

---

The National Security Council (NSC)

The National Security Council is an organization that was created by the National Security Act of 1947. The NSC is responsible for planning the defense policies of the United States. They also review existing policies and update them as needed. In addition the NSC directs the Central Intelligence Agency, a government organization that gathers information that could be harmful to the security of the United States. The NSC is part of the executive office of the president. The staff, which is made up of sixty-five civilian members, is headed by an executive secretary called the national security adviser. The other members of the staff are the president and vice president, the secretaries of state and defense, and the director of the Office of Emergency Planning.

---

cussing his work problems with his wife or family. Colin also tried to help ease tensions at the office by keeping a good sense of humor, and kidding around with his staff. People who worked for Colin found him even-tempered and willing to listen, but they always knew he was the boss.

One of Colin's biggest accomplishments as national security adviser was putting together a treaty between the United States and the Soviet Union to eliminate intermediate-range nuclear weapons. The

Soviet Union, a Communist country, had been an enemy of the U.S. since the end of World War II. The two countries had not actually engaged in war against each other, but they each feared that the other would attack. As a result, the two countries had been stockpiling nuclear weapons to use against each other.

With the Intermediate-Range Nuclear Forces (INF) treaty, both countries promised to destroy their intermediate-range missiles by 1990. For the first time, the Soviets also agreed to let United States officials inspect Soviet missile sites to make sure the missiles were destroyed. The Soviets would be allowed to inspect the U.S. missile sites as well. On December 8, 1987, after a three-day summit meeting in Washington, D.C., President Reagan and Soviet President Mikhail Gorbachev signed this agreement.

Colin's role in creating the treaty included determining how the missiles were going to be destroyed, and who would get to inspect the missile sites afterwards. He was also the person who briefed the international press on what had taken place during the summit. A short time later, Colin received the Distinguished Service Award for his outstanding contribution in this important foreign policy matter. The summit in Washington was only the first of seven international summits that Colin coordinated. These included two more summits between President Reagan and President Gorbachev that took place in 1988 in New York and Moscow.

In November 1988 Ronald Reagan finished his second and final term as president of the United States. Reagan's former vice-president, George Bush, was elected as the new president. Colin had the feeling that George Bush would probably want to choose his own national security adviser. This meant that Colin would soon have to give up the job.

On November 23, 1988 retired Air Force Lieutenant General Brent Scowcroft was named George Bush's new national security adviser. Colin's last day in office was a sad one. "I went home to watch the inauguration on TV," he said. "At 1:30 that afternoon, I absentmindedly picked up my White House phone to place a call. It [the line] was dead."

Colin, then fifty-one, began to think about what he might like to do next. Finally he decided to call up his friend and mentor, Army Chief of Staff General Carl Vuono, and ask him for a job—any job.

General Vuono had been hoping Colin would come back to the Army. He had been saving a job for

---

How to Tell the Rank of a U.S. Army Officer

Second Lieutenant	single gold bar
First Lieutenant	single silver bar
Captain	two silver bars
Major	gold oak leaf
Lieutenant Colonel	silver oak leaf
Colonel	silver eagle
Brigadier General	one silver star
Major General	two silver stars
Lieutenant General	three silver stars
General	four silver stars
General of the Army	five silver stars

---

him in case he did: the head of the Army's biggest single combat unit, known as Forces Command (ForsCom). General Vuono also wanted to award Colin his fourth star, making him the only black four-star general in the U.S. military.

Colin readily accepted the position. He would become one of ten United States military command-ers in chief (known as Cincs, pronounced "sinks").

Forces Command is the Army's single biggest command. As ForsCom commander, Colin's job was to make sure that one million active-duty soldiers, reservists, and National Guard troops were properly prepared for battle, if war ever erupted. It was a very important military position.

Colin and his family eagerly began packing for the move to Fort MacPherson, Georgia. They did not know they would have to turn around and head back to Washington, D.C., only six months later. Then something even greater would be in store for Colin.

5

The Chairman's First Challenge

On August 8, 1989 Secretary of Defense Dick Cheney ordered his secretary to get General Colin Powell into his office at once. Colin, who happened to be in Washington, D.C., at the time, hurried over to Cheney's office. It was in the Pentagon, the gigantic five-sided building complex in Arlington, Virginia, that houses America's main military headquarters.

Once Colin was seated in his office, Secretary Cheney quickly got to the point. He told Colin that Navy Admiral William Crowe, Jr., chairman of the Joint Chiefs of Staff, would be retiring in September. Colin was being seriously considered for the job. As the person holding the highest position in the United States military, the chairman is in charge of all of the other military service chiefs. The only two people with higher military authority are the secretary of defense and the president.

"Are you interested in the job?" Secretary Cheney asked Colin. "Is it something you want?"

Colin said he would like the job, but then added, "I do not seek the job. I'm happy where I am. If you pick someone else, I would not be upset at all. If you and the president want me, I'll do it."

Secretary Cheney returned to the White House and reported Colin's answers to President Bush. The president told Secretary Cheney that he approved of Colin's selection as chairman. The secretary telephoned Colin the following day with the news.

Colin took over the chairman position at midnight on October 1. His first day in office would be Monday, October 3. However, a crisis arose before the weekend was over.

For some time, the political situation in the Central American country of Panama had been creating problems for the American government. American influence had been important in Panama since the early 1900s, when the Panama Canal was built. The canal, which links the Atlantic and Pacific Oceans, remains an important trade and military strategic

Defense Secretary Cheney swears in Colin Powell as the twelfth chairman of the Joint Chiefs of Staff. Colin's wife, Alma, is holding the Bible. (AP/Wide World, 1989)

route today. Because of this, thousands of United States troops are stationed in Panama to help run and protect the canal. The Panama Canal will continue to be run by the United States until the year 2000, when it is scheduled to be turned over to Panamanian control.

In 1989 the Panamanian government was being led by General Manuel Antonio Noriega, who was also the head of Panama's armed forces, the

Panamanian Defense Forces (PDF). General Noriega had a reputation for being a brutal and corrupt military dictator. It was also suspected that under his direction, huge shipments of illegal drugs were being sold to the United States. The Bush administration wanted to see his political power taken away.

On May 7, 1989 free elections were held in Panama. The vote count indicated that General Noriega's opponent, Guillermo Endura, had won the election. Of course, Noriega did not want to give up his position as leader, so he announced to everyone that the election was not valid. The Panamanian people took to the streets in protest, shouting in Spanish, "Down with the pineapple!" This was their nickname for Noriega because of his pock-marked, acne-scarred face.

In response to the protests, Noriega's armed supporters, called the "Dignity Battalions" violently beat the protestors, including the opposition presidential and vice-presidential candidates. The two men being beaten by Noriega's Dignity Battalions were broadcast over and over again on American television.

The American government was not about to ignore the situation. The Pentagon had been developing a number of secret operations plans called Elaborate Maze for about a year. One of these plans was code-named Blue Spoon. It called for an offensive attack by the United States military against the PDF. This operation would be conducted from Panama by the local United States Army commander, the CincSouth.

However, the plans were undeveloped and the U.S. Military in Panama was avoiding conflict under President Bush's orders. On October 1, Colin's first day in office, rebel leaders in Panama contacted the United States and asked for military support to help them get rid of Noriega. President Bush was anxious to get Noriega out of Panama. But he listened when Colin urged him to watch things develop before taking any action. Colin thought that the events were moving too quickly for U.S. forces to do any good and he did not want to jeopardize the lives of American soldiers.

The rebels went after Noriega without U.S. backing. But the attempt was poorly planned and the rebels' leader was unreliable. They were soon squashed by Noriega's forces. Both politicians and the public saw the lack of American support as indecision on the part of the president and the new Joint Chiefs of Staff chairman. However, the criticism made

Colin more determined to devise a plan that would drive out the military leadership in Panama. He did not want to be unprepared again.

Before he could revise the plans, though, on October 3, 1989 Colin was formally inducted as chairman of the Joint Chiefs of Staff. Many of the Pentagon's twenty thousand employees stopped work just before three o'clock on that cool, sunny October day. They filled the giant parade grounds overlooking the Potomac River to watch the welcoming ceremony. The crowd cheered as Secretary Cheney led Colin to the reviewing stand.

When it was Colin's turn to speak, he described a painting of a church that hangs inside a stairwell at the Pentagon. "A large church," Colin said, "with bright sunlight streaming through a beautiful stained glass window. The church is empty except for a single family praying at the altar rail. The sunlight is falling on the family. There is a mother and father, and a young son and daughter, and the father is in uniform. You can sense from the painting that the family is praying together one last time before the father goes off to war. Every time I pass that painting a silent prayer comes to mind for all those who serve this nation in times of danger."

Colin knew from firsthand experience how terrible war could be, and how scary it was to send troops into battle. But as much as he hated the idea of sending soldiers like that father in the painting off to fight, he also felt that America required a strong military defense.

Colin believes in using a strategy called "deterrence" to keep peace in the world. This means that if the United States maintains a strong military force, other countries may be deterred, or discouraged, from starting major wars. Colin's inspiration came from an ancient Greek historian named Thucydides, who said, "Of all manifestations of power, restraint impresses men most." Colin liked this idea so much he placed it under the glass covering his desk at the Pentagon.

Colin also believes that if American forces are committed to battle, they should be sent off to fight only in numbers large enough to win. "By nature," Colin explains, "I'm very cautious about the use of the armed forces . . . putting lives on the line. But when it's clear we're going to use them, well, let's use them."

Colin spent the first few weeks reviewing the Elaborate Maze plans in the event he had to put American lives on the line. After looking at Blue

Spoon, Colin wanted the plans for the operation reworked to emphasize surprise and speed. He also wanted the attacks to occur under cover of darkness by soldiers using high-tech night vision goggles.

Planning for Panama had to take a backseat at the end of November when a new crisis arose. On November 30, a one-thousand man rebel force had seized two air bases in the Philippines. Someone was plotting to overthrow President Corazon Aquino's government. There were also reports that her palace was being bombed by planes. The U.S. has several large military bases in the Phillipines. If the government were to fall, the new leaders might try to force the Americans out. This would jeopardize the balance of power in the Pacific region.

Upon hearing the news, Colin immediately went up to Secretary Cheney's office, carrying site maps and intelligence reports. He told the secretary that the situation in the Philippines was still unclear. Then, after reviewing the latest information, Colin went home for dinner.

As the evening wore on, a committee of deputies from different government agencies continued to monitor the crisis. At one point, the Filipino defense minister requested American military intervention.

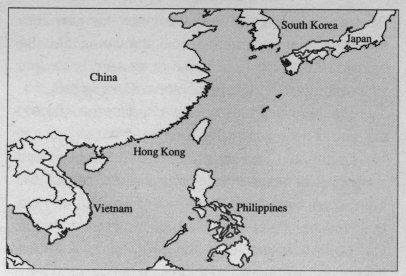

Philippines and Southeast Asia

According to official reports, President Aquino herself wanted the U.S. to use their F-4 fighter planes based in the Phillipines to bomb the rebel air bases. It looked like things were getting very serious.

By eleven o'clock that night, Colin was back at the Pentagon for a National Security Council meeting which would be conducted by video. Vice President Dan Quayle was put in charge of the meeting because President Bush was on his way to Malta for a summit meeting with Mikhail Gorbachev.

As reports of rebel bombing began to come in, Colin took his seat in the Crisis Situation Room at the

Pentagon's National Military Command Center. Deputy Secretary Eagleburger told the committee he believed American forces had to be sent in to deal with the conflict in the Philippines. "This is a democratic government that we have sponsored," he explained. "There really should be no debate."

By this the secretary meant that the U.S. had supported democratic elections in the Phillippines. The people had voted in President Aquino, and the U.S. had then helped the Filipinos to force Ferdinand Marcos, the dictator who had been controlling their country for twenty years, to give up his power.

Most of the committee seemed to agree that the U.S. military needed to somehow intervene in support of President Aquino's government. Still, Colin was cautious. He felt that some of the reports from the Philippines were unclear. The Filipinos might be panicking and asking for American military intervention too soon. The bombing they were requesting required precise target information. "You don't call up a twenty-two-year-old or twenty-three-year-old kid and say, just go bomb here," Colin warned.

Then he came up with a plan. He suggested that American military pilots should first fly over the captured Filipino air bases in an attempt to scare off the rebels. If the rebel planes started to taxi down the runway in preparation for takeoff, then the U.S. pilots should fire some warning shots in front of them. Finally, if the rebel planes did lift off, then the American pilots should shoot them down. Colin said he hoped the earlier warnings would deter the rebel aircraft from taking off because then the mission could be accomplished without having to really fight.

The committee agreed with Colin that this sounded like the best plan. Vice President Quayle decided to call the president on Air Force One to discuss it with him. The vice president described Colin's plan to President Bush, who then approved it.

By 1:30 A.M. Washington, D.C., time, the United States Air Force had launched its planes which flew repeatedly over the rebel air bases. The U.S. planes were advanced F-4 fighter-bomber jets. The rebels were using T-28s, old World War II propeller planes. Early reports to the Pentagon said that there were no T-28s in the air or any new rebel bombing.

At 2:30 A.M. Vice President Quayle telephoned President Aquino. He wanted to make sure that she still wanted the U.S. to continue according to plan, which included bombing the rebels. When Mrs. Aquino said yes, Quayle replied, "We're with you."

While Quayle was speaking with President Aquino, Colin was trying to get in touch with the defense minister of the Phillipines, Fidel Ramos, to get an update on the situation. Ramos told Colin that the rebels were no longer able to get their planes off the ground. Even though they had bombed the presidential palace, President Aquino had no intention of leaving. Colin said he thought the U.S. plan was working. Ramos agreed, and said that the Phillipine government appreciated the American efforts.

By 5:30 A.M., Colin and the rest of the committee concluded that the rebels had been totally defeated. The crisis was over, and Colin had played a big role in solving it. His method was military, but no one had actually had to fight. Everyone thought he and his staff had performed brilliantly. Exhausted but relieved, Colin went home to sleep.

6

Crisis in Panama

On the night of December 16, 1989, Colin's private phone rang at home. An off-duty Marine in Panama had been shot and killed by the PDF.

No American soldier had been killed by the Panamanian Defense Forces before. Colin knew that this meant Panama had become a crisis situation again. He immediately called Secretary Cheney at home. "It's starting to build," he said.

The Marine who had been shot was Lieutenant Robert Paz. He had been one of four off-duty officers, all of whom were unarmed and wearing civilian clothes. They had gone out for dinner in Panama City and had made a wrong turn onto a street near PDF headquarters. Their car had been stopped by armed soldiers at a PDF roadblock, and the driver had tried to speed away from the scene. The PDF soldiers had then opened fire on the car, fatally wounding Paz.

By 6:00 A.M. the next day, another disturbing report came into the Pentagon. There had been a second incident at the same PDF checkpoint. A Navy lieutenant named Adam J. Curtis and his wife, Bonnie, had been stopped there about a half hour before the shooting, and asked to wait for their identification to be cleared. While they were waiting, they happened to witness the shooting of Lieutenant Paz. Members of the PDF then blindfolded the couple with masking tape, and brought them to PDF headquarters where they were interrogated and verbally abused. Lieutenant Curtis was also beaten.

After four hours, the Curtises were finally released. They returned to the U.S. Naval Station after two o'clock in the morning, and reported what had happened to them.

Meanwhile, General Noriega had issued a statement that the shooting incident had been the fault of the four American officers. He claimed the American officers had broken through the PDF checkpoint and shot at the headquarters building, wounding three Panamanians. According to General Kelly, this report was ridiculous. Noriega had been overheard on the radio and telephone trying to come up with phony stories that would make it seem as if the Americans were to blame.

Colin called CincSouth's General Maxwell Thurman on a special, secure telephone line. He was ready to spring into action. General Thurman already had his more than 13,000 troops at the second-highest state of combat readiness. He told Colin he thought it was time that Operation Blue Spoon be put into action. He felt that Panama was provoking the United States into a fight.

Colin, however, was not yet fully convinced that it was time to go to war. He told General Thurman, "I've got to go brief Cheney. I'll get back to you later."

Colin and Secretary Cheney discussed how to handle what had happened in Panama. Both agreed that the murder and harassment of Americans living in Panama could not be permitted to occur. They had to do something. Colin suggested calling the Joint Chiefs together, to make sure they were all in agreement before talking to anyone in the White House.

The four chiefs met Colin at his house that Sunday morning. Colin updated them on the Blue Spoon plan, and told them that both he and Secretary

Colin and the Joint Chiefs of Staff in 1991. Left to right: Gen. Merrill A. McPeak, Chief of Staff of the Air Force; Adm. Frank B. Kelso II, Chief of Naval Operations; Gen. Alfred M. Gray, Commandant of the Marine Corps; Gen. Carl E. Vuono, Chief of Staff of the Army; Gen. Powell, Chairman; and Adm. David E. Jeremiah, Vice Chairman. (Courtesy of the Defense Department)

Cheney wanted to recommend carrying out the plan to President Bush later that afternoon. Colin assured the chiefs that the operation was designed for a quick victory. A total of 24,000 American troops would be fighting against the 16,000-member Panamanian Defense Forces, which included only 3,500 combat-capable soldiers. The Americans had better equipment, technology for fighting at night, and better-trained soldiers.

Colin still wanted the service chiefs' advice about what he should tell the president. When the meeting was over, all four chiefs backed Colin.

President Bush also agreed with Colin that Operation Blue Spoon seemed to be the solution to the problem in Panama. After hearing a summary of the Joint Chiefs' discussion, the president said, "Okay, let's go." The operation was set to begin at 1:00 A.M. on Wednesday, December 20.

Just before midnight on Tuesday, December 19, Colin arrived in the Crisis Situation Room. He was ready to begin the operation, which had been renamed Operation Just Cause. Because of a security leak in Panama, the PDF had found out about the American attack scheduled for 1:00 A.M. General Thurman decided that the operation had to take place earlier than was originally planned. It was important that the Americans not lose the element of surprise. Army Lieutenant General Carl W. Stiner, commander of the Army's Eighteenth Airborne Corps, told General Thurman that his troops could manage to launch the attack fifteen minutes early, but not before.

President Bush arrived in the Oval Office at the White House just around the time the operation began. A few minutes after 1:00 A.M., Secretary Cheney joined Colin and General Kelly in the Crisis Situation Room. For the next few hours, the country's leaders listened to a series of up-to-the-minute progress reports. They gradually learned that Noriega's headquarters had been destroyed by American forces, Panama's key military targets had been captured, and much of the organized PDF resistance had been stopped. While this was good news, there was bad news, too. General Manuel Noriega was still at large. And there had been several American casualties.

At around 7:00 A.M., President Bush addressed the nation on television. He described the Panama invasion to the American people. He explained that, to his mind, the Panamanian Defense Force's threats and attacks upon six American citizens in Panama represented a danger to the 35,000 Americans who were living in that country. He reminded the American people of the "horrible pictures" from the previous spring of Noriega's opposition candidates being brutally beaten. He then assured the country that he had decided to take military action in Panama only after realizing that there was no other solution.

Immediately following the president's address, Colin and Secretary Cheney held a televised briefing and press conference at the Pentagon. When Colin stood in front of the television cameras, he began his report with an account of success. U.S. forces had captured a Panamanian jail, he said, and freed nearly fifty political prisoners. Americans had succeeded in securing the country's electrical distribution center as well as the very important Madden Dam. They had also defeated a PDF infantry company, taken the Bridge of the Americas across the canal, secured the area around Howard Air Force Base, and knocked out the PDF Navy.

"We have not yet located the general," Colin reluctantly admitted, referring to Noriega, "but he is now a fugitive and will be treated as such." Then Colin went on to compliment the United States military for doing its job so efficiently. "We all deeply regret the loss of American life," Colin explained, "but that's sometimes necessary in pursuit of our national interests and in the fight for democracy." Preliminary information revealed that nine Americans were killed in action and thirty-nine were wounded.

By December 21, almost all of the main goals of

Operation Just Cause had been achieved, except one—the capture of General Manuel Noriega.

The United States announced it would pay a reward of one million dollars to anyone who offered the government information that might lead to his arrest. But Noriega still had a few tricks up his sleeve.

On the afternoon of December 24—Christmas Eve—a car drove up to the home of the Vatican's representative in Panama, known as the Papal Nuncio. Inside that car was General Noriega. Carrying two AK-47 rifles over his shoulder, Noriega got out of the car, entered the Nuncio's residence, and asked for political asylum. If granted, this would mean that for as long as he remained on church property, he was under the protection of the Catholic church, and no government could touch him.

Noriega's clever escape strategy did not stop the American government from pursuing him, however. General Stiner phoned General Kelly on the Pentagon hot line. He asked him for new combat rules that would permit his forces to enter the Nuncio's home if asked to by church officials, or if shooting started. General Kelly passed the request to Colin and Secretary Cheney, who both approved it within the hour.

Colin and Dick Cheney brief reporters on events in Panama in December 1989. (UPI/Bettman)

On Wednesday, December 27, General Thurman and General Stiner ordered some of their troops to blast the Nuncio's residence with ear-splitting heavy metal rock music. This was to keep anyone from overhearing the Army's negotiations with the Papal Nuncio, and also to unnerve Noriega. People who lived nearby said the music was so loud it could be heard for blocks. Meanwhile, other troops had been ordered to act as if they were preparing the building for an assault. Tall grass and brush in the area was cut down to improve vision. Streetlights were shot out and barbed wire was unrolled in the streets. Helicopters landed and unloaded troops, while tanks and personnel carriers blocked the streets. The Army meant business. But General Noriega did not budge.

Then, suddenly, at 8:44 P.M. on Wednesday, January 3, 1990, Manuel Noriega walked out of the Nuncio's residence in his military uniform and surrendered. Apparently he had misunderstood the conditions under which he was to be taken into custody. He thought the Americans were going to treat him as a head of state, or at least as a prisoner of war. Instead they just slapped a set of handcuffs on him as if he were any common criminal. This made Noriega furious. He began shouting and cursing at the Papal Nuncio, who just kept on blessing him as he was being led into the helicopter.

After announcing the capture of Noriega in a press conference, Bush added, "I want to express the special thanks of our nation to those servicemen who were wounded and to the families of those who gave their lives. Their sacrifice has been a noble cause and will never be forgotten."

The military action in Panama had given the

American soldiers surround the Vatican Embassy in Panama in January 1990 to capture General Noriega. (Christopher Morris/Black Star)

United States and its armed forces the first quick and unmistakable victory in battle since the failure of the war in Vietnam.

7

The War in the Gulf

Colin faced another major conflict shortly after the Panama invasion. This time the crisis occurred in the Persian Gulf.

Saddam Hussein, the president of Iraq, had been arguing with Sheik Jabir al-Ahmad al-Sabah, the leader of the neighboring country of Kuwait, over oil prices and land boundaries since 1989. To begin with, Saddam complained that oil prices on the world market were too low because Kuwait, which held ten percent of the world's oil reserves, was producing too much oil. When oil was abundant, other countries were not willing to pay as much for it, and the prices were kept low. Saddam believed that oil was the Middle East's most valuable resource, and he desperately needed large profits from oil so that he could pay back his huge debts from the Iran-Iraq War.

Saddam also insisted that he wanted to take back some land that had been a part of Iraq's Basra Province until the British had granted Kuwait its independence in 1961. The Kuwaitis did not want to return the land to Iraq, and refused to give in to Saddam's demands.

But Saddam would not take no for an answer. He began to gather his military forces along the Kuwaiti border. Not only did Saddam roll in his tanks, but his communications, artillery, and airpower units also were maneuvered into place. Soon nearly one-hundred thousand Iraqi troops were poised and ready to strike. And on August 2, 1990, they did.

That evening Colin and Secretary of Defense Cheney each received telephone calls at home from Rear Admiral Bill Owens, commander of the Sixth Fleet, who was stationed in the Mediterranean. He reported that the Iraqi forces had crossed the border into Kuwait and hundreds of battle tanks were racing toward Kuwait City, the nation's capital. Both men decided to remain at home that night and wait for updates. Admiral David Jeremiah, vice chairman of the Joint Chiefs of Staff, went to the Pentagon to

Oil Makes the World Go 'Round

Since ancient times animal and vegetable oils have been used for lighting, lubrication, and for medicines. In the 1850s it was learned that oil from under the ground was excellent for lighting and for lubricating machinery. The first well to pump oil was built in Pennsylvania in 1859. Soon the rush was on. People were prospecting for oil throughout the United States. In 1865 John D. Rockefeller founded Standard Oil, which eventually controlled most of the production and refining throughout the country. Rockefeller went on to become the richest man in America. With the invention of the internal combustion engine, the need for "black gold" grew. Automobiles, ships, and the new airplanes could not function without it. In the 1920s oil was discovered in the Middle East, particularly in Saudi Arabia, Kuwait, and Bahrain. As the black, sticky liquid became more and more necessary for modern life (plastic is made from oil), its value increased. Warfare became increasingly dependent on oil because ships, planes, and tanks use fuel in enormous quantities. This means that countries with large underground supplies can become very wealthy and powerful. But if one country or group of countries control too much oil, others may feel threatened. Nations will even fight wars to obtain oil, as Japan did during World War II. When Iraq invaded Kuwait in 1990, one of the main reasons was the large oil supply that lies beneath the desert sands.

monitor the crisis, along with General Kelly.

For most of the night, General Kelly kept one eye on the classified military information that was being transmitted to the Pentagon over a large video screen. The other eye he kept glued to a television set tuned into CNN, the twenty-four-hour cable news channel. The general wanted to keep track of the reports that were being broadcast to the public. Colin might want to take steps to correct those reports, if he felt they were wrong in any way.

General Kelly also stayed in touch with Army General H. Norman Schwarzkopf throughout the night. General Schwarzkopf was the Cinc in charge of the United States Central Command, whose territory included the Middle East and Southwest Asia. A big, burly man of six-foot-three and 240 pounds, Schwarzkopf was called "Stormin' Norman" and "The Bear" by his troops, and was considered tough. He was a top-notch commander, and he knew the Middle East well. General Schwarzkopf had already been instructed by Colin to draft the plans for possible U.S. responses to any move by Iraq against Kuwait, so General Kelly wanted Schwarzkopf's input on all developments in the crisis.

When President Bush heard about what was

The President of Iraq

Saddam Hussein was born in 1937 to a peasant family, but his parents died when he was very young. As a young man he joined the Baath political party, which supported the idea of unity among all Arabs. In 1959 he was part of a group that tried to assassinate Iraq's dictator. The plot failed and Saddam had to escape to Egypt. When the Baaths seized power in 1968, Saddam returned and became a powerful leader of the party. In 1979 he took control of the country and immediately began to kill and imprison people who might oppose him. With a steady flow of money from the sale of oil, Saddam built up the Iraqi army and started a long, bloody war with neighboring Iran. He did not hesitate to use poison gas on both his enemies and his own people and is reported to have personally killed many political enemies. Under Saddam Hussein most Iraqi people live in terror.

happening in the Persian Gulf, he said he wanted something to be done about it right away. He issued a statement condemning the invasion and calling for "the immediate and unconditional withdrawal of all Iraqi forces."

Saddam Hussein did not listen.

Early the next morning, the National Security Council met to discuss possible diplomatic and mili-

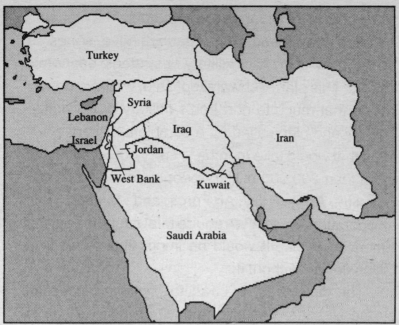

The Middle East

tary solutions to the growing crisis in the Persian Gulf. Having taken over Kuwait, Iraq now held twenty percent of the world's oil reserves. Saddam could easily raise world oil prices if he wanted to, which would be very bad for the American economy. If Saddam also decided to conquer Saudi Arabia, Kuwait's southwestern neighbor, he would control forty percent of the world's oil. President Bush strongly felt that this could not be allowed to happen.

General Schwarzkopf presented two different

plans of military action to the president. The first plan included the United States launching a series of limited attacks on Iraqi military or strategic economic targets. This plan, Schwarzkopf said, would probably not do that much to hurt Iraq's military or economy. The second plan called for a complete military operation that would take months to carry out, and involve more than 200,000 military people from all four services: the Army, Navy, Air Force, and Marines. Such an operation would also require total support from the American public. It would be impossible to wage a full-scale war without it.

The diplomatic, or peaceful, options discussed by the National Security Council included trying to pressure Saddam to leave Kuwait by cutting him off from all trade with other countries. These kinds of sanctions (in this case, "sanctions" mean a type of penalty) might hurt Iraq's economy so badly that it would have to give in to the world's demands.

The NSC decided that, for the moment, waiting for the economic sanctions to work was the best approach. If the sanctions succeeded in convincing Saddam to leave Kuwait, then the mission would be accomplished without any fighting. If they did not succeed, then at least the United States military would have had the time it needed to prepare for war.

While the president was waiting for the results of the sanctions, he decided he was not taking any chances. Within days after Saddam's army moved into Kuwait, America began sending its first ground forces and warplanes to Saudi Arabia to block a possible Iraqi invasion of that country. The United States also sent Navy ships to the Persian Gulf region to stop—by force, if necessary—any goods or supplies from being carried in or out of Iraqi ports. Operation Desert Shield had begun.

But Saddam did not back down. Instead he increased the number of his troops in Kuwait, and announced that the country was no longer an independent nation; it was now part of Iraq. Many Kuwaitis were forced from their homes, tortured, and killed as Iraqi troops pushed their way deep into the country. Thousands of Americans and Europeans who were living in Kuwait were rounded up by the Iraqis and taken hostage. Many were taken to important military and industrial sites in Iraq. The Iraqis hoped to prevent attacks on these sites by placing the hostages there as "human shields."

The rest of the world decided it was not going to stand by and watch. By order of the United Nations

Colin meeting with General H. Norman Schwarzkopf in Saudi Arabia. (AP/Wide World)

Security Council, representative forces from other countries soon joined the American troops in the desert.

Once President Bush had made the decision to deploy America's forces to the Persian Gulf, Colin and Secretary Cheney pushed the operation through with amazing speed. In less than twenty-four hours after they were ordered to leave, units from the Eighty-second Airborne Division arrived in Saudi Arabia. The heavily armed Twenty-fourth Infantry Division was on its way by ship within a week. In three months, 180,000 people, seven billion pounds of equipment, as well as hundreds of tanks and airplanes would be shipped halfway around the world.

As Colin carried out his orders from the president, he began to wonder where all this buildup of forces was going to lead. So far, the only stated mission of the troops was to stand firm and attempt to deter Saddam from invading Saudi Arabia. If deterrence failed, then their job would be to defend Saudi Arabia against Saddam's attack. At the rate things were going, however, the United States would have 250,000 troops stationed in the Persian Gulf by December 1—a lot of soldiers and equipment to keep just sitting around in the desert. What if Saddam did not invade Saudi Arabia? Colin wondered. How long did President Bush want all those Americans to stay there? What exactly did he want them to do? Colin advised the president he needed to make those decisions, and it needed to be soon.

President Bush and Colin were feeling pressure from all sides. The press wanted more information about the military buildup. Congress kept reminding the president that he needed their permission before declaring war on Saddam. As more and more military units were called overseas, families across America were being torn apart. Even General Schwarzkopf kept telephoning Colin, asking him for hints as to what might happen next. Were they going to continue their defensive mission? Or did the president want the forces to do more?

"Norm," Colin kept telling him, "I'm working on it."

It wasn't long before General Schwarzkopf got his answer. President Bush finally did decide to change the military's mission—from the defense of Saudi Arabia to the liberation of Kuwait.

From a military point of view, Colin thought these two missions were as different as night and day. Trying to scare off Iraq from invading Saudi Arabia was one thing—but forcing its large, powerful army to leave was one of the hardest things his soldiers could have possibly been asked to do.

Colin wanted to make sure the president had fully considered every option besides going to war with Saddam. Colin was in favor of keeping the economic sanctions going, since they did seem to be weakening Iraq. He also suggested a military strategy, but not an offensive one. Called "containment," Colin's strategy meant using the U.N. forces to surround and "strangle" Iraq by completely cutting it off from any contact with the outside world. Colin explained to the president that this strategy would take longer, maybe even a year or two, but it would probably work, and no blood would have to be shed.

President Bush did not want to follow the containment policy. Colin had not wanted to go to war, but he would back the president. And once this decision was made, Colin believed that the allies should "strike suddenly, decisively, and in sufficient force to resolve the matter." He wanted to do everything in his power to make sure the allied forces won.

In late November the United Nations set a deadline for Iraq's withdrawal from Kuwait: January 15, 1991. After that, the U.N. decided that its members would be free to use any means, including military force, to drive Iraq out. Colin went to Saudi Arabia to make sure that General Schwarzkopf had everything he needed in case of war.

He also knew that Christmas was coming and the troops would be homesick. He visited many of the soldiers and assured them that their work was needed and appreciated. "I know what it's like to be away from your family for the holidays," he said. "But this is important work. Stay with us; we'll take care of your families and get you home as fast as we can."

Colin talks with the troops in Saudi Arabia. (Sygma)

On January 12, while some antiwar protestors around the country shouted "No blood for oil!" and "No war for Bush!", the United States Congress met to vote on whether the president would be permitted to direct American troops to launch an offensive attack on Iraq. By sixty-seven votes in the House of Representatives, and five votes in the Senate, Congress did grant the president the authority to use military force in the Persian Gulf.

Tuesday, January 15, would be the first of three moonless nights in Iraq and Kuwait. In past wars, pilots had called the full moon "the bomber's moon," because they needed the extra light to see their targets. In this war, a pitch-black night was what the military commanders wanted. Infrared devices and laser-guided bombs would enable the pilots to see and hit their targets in the dark. Moonlight would only expose them to their enemies.

The U.N. deadline of January 15 was set for midnight, American Eastern Standard Time. But because time zones around the world are different, in Baghdad this would be eight o'clock the following morning. The allied forces would have to wait for nightfall on January 16 before the war could begin.

Colin knew that he and General Schwarzkopf had done all they could. They hoped that the operation that was about to start would cause little damage and loss of life. At Colin's insistence, the air campaign was only going to destroy two of the six bridges inside the city of Baghdad. Colin did not think it fair or right to destroy Iraq so totally.

After thirty-two years in the military, Colin was facing his ultimate challenge. He thought of the troops; many of the soldiers were very young, and now the war was in their hands. In the quiet of his office, as Colin waited for the bombing of Baghdad to begin, he wondered, "How many will not come back?"

Colin and President Bush consult with General Schwarzkopf by phone in the Oval Office of the White House. (David Valdez/The White House)

Just before 1:00 A.M. in the Middle East, reporters at United States air bases in Saudi Arabia began describing the wave of jets that were taking off. People listening to the reports could hear the thunder of the engines in the background. The planes headed north toward Kuwait and Iraq. With the departure of these jets, Operation Desert Shield became Operation Desert Storm.

American and allied planes pounded targets throughout Iraq and Kuwait around the clock. In the first thirty hours of the war, they completed approxi-

---

War on TV

The television networks had been preparing to cover a war in the Persian Gulf for five months. The first attack came during the evening news. CNN correspondents reported the initial bombings from the Al Rasheed Hotel in Baghdad. Other stations showed correspondents wearing gas masks during their report while air raid sirens wailed in the background. ABC, NBC, and CBS cut out regular programming to bring information about the war. Dick Cheney and Colin often referred to CNN during their press briefings. Even Saddam Hussein tuned in to CNN. Because of the continuous coverage by television, the Persian Gulf War became known as "The TV War."

---

mately two thousand air missions.

Saddam was not about to take the allied attack lying down. Instead he came up with a whole new strategy. He began firing deadly Scud missiles on the cities of Tel Aviv and Haifa in Israel. Israel had not been a part of the conflict up to this point, but by attacking the Israelis, Saddam hoped to draw them into the war. He believed that the Arab nations who had sided with the United States against him would return to his side if he were fighting a war against Israel. But fortunately, the missiles did little damage and Israel did not respond to Saddam's attacks.

Meanwhile Colin was trying to manage the war from Washington, D.C. Besides all of his behind-the-scenes military planning and decision-making for Desert Shield, he was briefing the press and the public about how the war was progressing. It was up to Colin to reassure the public that the military knew exactly what they were doing. He firmly stated that everything was under control and proceeding according to schedule. Handling the press became a very important part of Colin's job during the Gulf War.

CNN, the cable-TV news channel, was broadcasting stories about the war twenty-four-hours a day. The military released a tape of Scud missiles hitting their targets. The public saw bombs sailing through the open doors of a bunker in which an Iraqi missile was stored, and watched another missile shoot down the air shaft of a building. The fuzz on the screen that followed was the bomb's explosion.

Colin's military philosophy of striking suddenly and decisively was effective in Operation Desert Storm. By February 27, after only forty-two days, the United States and the allied forces had destroyed Saddam's army and liberated Kuwait. All of the military commanders were hailed as national heroes—

President Bush hugs Colin at a joint session of Congress in March 1991. (Reuters/Bettman)

but especially Colin Powell, who had brilliantly led his country to victory.

On Monday, April 15, 1991, Colin returned to his old neighborhood in the South Bronx for a visit. He received a genuine hero's welcome. The mayor of New York City had declared it "Colin Powell Day," and thousands of Bronx residents wearing yellow ribbons and waving American flags turned out in the rain to applaud the famous general.

Colin was excited about revisiting his old high school, and talking with the students there. And the

These are the rules that have helped General Powell in his Army career:

1. It ain't as bad as you think. It will look better in the morning.
2. Get mad, then get over it.
3. Avoid having your ego so close to your position that when your position falls, your ego goes with it.
4. It can be done!
5. Be careful what you choose. You may get it.
6. You can't make someone else's choices. You shouldn't let someone else make yours.
7. Check small things.
8. Share credit.
9. Remain calm. Be kind.

students were eager to meet him, too. "There's no kidding about this man," said one boy admiringly. "He's the real thing."

At Morris High School the auditorium was packed with fans. When Colin addressed the crowd, he said that he had worked hard to become a general and the Joint Chiefs chairman. He had stayed in school, even when he found it difficult or boring. Colin urged the students to finish their own education and make something of their lives. "Stick with it," the general said. "I'm giving you an order."

COLIN POWELL

As chairman of the Joint Chiefs of Staff, Colin Powell is the highest-ranking black military officer in United States history. On May 23, 1991 he was reappointed by President Bush to a second two-year term.

Quick Facts

The United States Armed Forces

The United States armed forces are made up of five branches. The chairman of the Joint Chiefs of Staff oversees the chief of each of the military services, except for the Coast Guard.

- **The Army** makes up the United States' armed land forces. It is the oldest military service in the country. The Army was formed in 1775, and its first commander was George Washington.

- **The Air Force** was originally a part of the Army and was formed to provide air support to ground troops. The Air Force became a separate branch in 1947.

- **The Navy** is the country's sea forces. In World War II, the U.S. Navy dominated the Pacific Ocean with their heavily gunned battleships, aircraft carriers, and submarines.

- **The Marine Corps** is a service that operates as part of the Navy. But it is actually a separate force with its own member of the Joint Chiefs, the commandant of the Marine Corps. The Marines have their own armor, aviation, and artillery units and specialize in amphibious attacks.

- **The Coast Guard** was founded in 1790. It is a special seagoing force that is part of the Navy during wartime. In peacetime it serves under the U.S. Treasury Department. The Coast Guard protects the U.S. coastline from drug smugglers, and controls water pollution, enforces navigational rules, and aids ships and aircraft in distress.

Chronology

1937   Colin is born on April 5.

1954   Colin enters City College and joins the ROTC.

1958   Colin graduates from City College at the top of his ROTC class.
        On June 9 he is commissioned as a second lieutenant.

1962   Colin marries Alma Vivian Johnson on August 25.
        In December Colin goes to Vietnam as a military adviser.

1963   Michael Powell is born.
        Colin is injured in Vietnam. He earns a Bronze Star for Valor.

1966   Linda Powell is born.

1968   Colin is sent back to Vietnam.
        Colin's helicopter crashes and he rescues the other soldiers. He is awarded a Soldier's Medal for his heroism.

1969   Colin returns to the U.S. and attends graduate
        school at George Washington University.

1971   Annemarie Powell is born.

1972   Colin is chosen to be a White House fellow.

1981   Colin is made a military assistant to the
        secretary of defense.

1986   Colin leaves Washington to command the V
        Corps in West Germany.

1987   Colin is named deputy national security ad-
        viser.
        Colin's son Michael is seriously injured in a
        jeep accident in Germany.
        In November Colin is named the national
        security adviser.

1989   In April Colin becomes commander in chief of
        Forces Command at Fort MacPherson.
        On October 3 Colin is named chairman of the
        Joint Chiefs of Staff.
        On November 30 two U.S. airbases in the

Phillipines are seized by rebel forces.

Operation Just Cause starts in Panama on December 20.

1990   Iraq invades Kuwait on August 2.

1991   On January 16 the U.S. launches an air assault on Iraq and Operation Desert Storm begins.

The war ends on February 27.

Index

About the Authors

Jonathan Everston is an author of children's fiction and nonfiction. He earned his B.A. in English at Siena College and currently resides in Putnam Valley, New York.

Andrea Raab is a writer and freelance editor. Her most recent work is *In the Men's House: An Inside Account of Life in the Army by One of West Point's First Female Graduates*, co-written with Cpt. Carol Barkalow. Ms. Raab lives in New York City.